Jeannette A Grant

Through Evangeline's Country

Jeannette A Grant

Through Evangeline's Country

ISBN/EAN: 9783337210823

Printed in Europe, USA, Canada, Australia, Japan

Cover: Foto ©Andreas Hilbeck / pixelio.de

More available books at **www.hansebooks.com**

THROUGH EVANGELINE'S

COUNTRY

By JEANNETTE A. GRANT

ILLUSTRATED

"*Then he beheld, in a dream, once more the home of his
  childhood;
Green Acadian meadows, with sylvan rivers among them
Village and mountain and woodlands; and walking
  under their shadow,
As in the days of her youth, Evangeline rose in his vision.*"

BOSTON
JOSEPH KNIGHT COMPANY
1894

CONTENTS.

                                                  PAGE

PART I. *A Bit of History.*
    A Bit of Acadian History . 3

PART II. *The Acadia of To-day.*
    Chapter I. The Border Land, Yarmouth . 19
    Chapter II. By Saint Mary's Bay . . 25
        (Meteghan, Church Point.)

PART III. *Old Acadian Haunts.*
    Chapter I. Annapolis Royal . . . 57
        (Old Port Royal of the French.)
    Chapter II. In the Aunapolis Valley . . 66

PART IV. *The Poet's Acadia.*
    Chapter I. The Cornwallis Valley . 79
    Chapter II. Grand Pré 89

LIST OF ILLUSTRATIONS.

	PAGE
Evangeline, from a painting by Edwin Douglass . . . *Frontispiece.*	
Map of Evangeline's Country . .	v
Old Magazine at Annapolis .	3
Jacques Cartier	8
Entrance to Annapolis Basin . .	9
Samuel Champlain . . .	10
Halifax — View from Citadel . .	11
Near Annapolis Basin . . .	16
Yarmouth . .	19
Yarmouth Harbor .	21
Near Yarmouth . .	24
Digby	25
Byway near Digby . .	26
A Nova Scotia Cottage . .	33
Lighthouse, Saint Mary's Bay . .	49
Railway Bridge at Bear River . .	51
On the Way to Annapolis	57
Evening Shadows in the Acadian Land . .	59
Fragment of Old French Fort at Annapolis . .	62

	PAGE
Scenery near Annapolis	63
Apple Blossoms, Annapolis Valley	66
Apple Orchard, Annapolis Valley	71
Annapolis River	73
"Aground in the shallow River lay a Schooner"	76
Orchard in Bloom	79
Apple picking	80
Wolfville, not far from Grand Pré	81
Minas Basin — Blomidon in the Distance	83
"A Vessel lay on the Stocks"	86
Cutting through an Orchard	88
The Gaspereau Valley	89
Grand Pré Village, Home of Evangeline	91
Old Blacksmith Forge, Grand Pré	93
Old Willows — Grand Pré	95
"Away to the northward Blomidon rose"	97
Old Acadian Graveyard, Gaspereau	99

PART I.

A BIT OF HISTORY.

"*List to the mournful tradition still sung by the pines of the forest.*"

A BIT OF ACADIAN HISTORY.

WHILE lovers love and hearts are true, the story of Evangeline will never lose its interest. As long as the pages of history find readers, the record of the expulsion of the French inhabitants of *Acadie* will never cease to stir the sympathies and awake the indignation of him who reads. Whatever be the point of view, that struggling fragment of a nation, fighting for existence against fearful odds, treasuring in its heart an ideal king and mother country, stands out pathetically clear from its sombre background.

No one can study the history of the

French colonists in North America without pity for their lot and admiration for their steadfastness. Like wayward children deprived of parental oversight, they forgot the Golden Rule, and retaliated even to the uttermost when assailed; but by so doing they thought to vindicate not only their personal rights, but the honor of France and the majesty of their king. Alas for their mistaken zeal! That king had little thought for these far-away colonists, and but small appreciation of their loyalty, unless it showed itself in the form of revenue for the royal coffers. Moreover, the affairs of France were in sad disorder, and her monarchs lived in fear of assassination at home, and in deadly feud with their neighbors. Treaty after treaty was signed, and the colony of *Acadie* was given now to France and now to England, with as little concern as a man is given or taken on a checker-board.

Great worldly wisdom would be required by that colonist who to-day is a subject of France, and to-morrow finds that against his will he has been transformed into a subject of England, to enable him to be faithful in both conditions. The Acadians were not worldly wise; they were a simple-hearted people, who believed what their priests told them, and were proud of being French subjects. Loyalty was a striking characteristic among them, and it is but a poor kind of loyalty that can change the object of its fidelity in a day, or even in a year. Compulsory loyalty, if such an anomaly can exist, is a weak substitute for that which is freely given. It is no wonder then that the British governors of Acadia were dissatisfied with the semblance of allegiance which had been wrung from the French subjects of their English sovereign.

It was not until the faithful colonists had learned the futility of appeal to their French king, and had suffered much from their misplaced confidence, that they were able at last to see the wisdom of striving to become loyal subjects of the monarch into whose power their destiny had given them. To-day the Acadian French of Nova Scotia are considered good citizens, who desire the advancement of the Province, for whose possession their ancestors endured so much. They have a romantic attachment for the land of their birth, where so many tender memories of the past survive. As a people they are united by the strongest ties, a common ancestry, a common religion, and common traditions.

The historical facts which led up to the climax known as the expulsion of 1755 are briefly as follows: —

In the year 1497, five years after the great discovery by Columbus, John and Sebastian Cabot, in the employ of Henry the Seventh of England, visited the eastern shores of North America in the vicinity of Labrador. No settlements were made, but the mere discovery gave England a slight claim to the region.

Three years later, in 1500, a Portuguese adventurer, Gaspar de Cortereal, reached Labrador and spent some time in following the coast northward, for the objec' of all these early navigators was to find a northwest passage to India.

After four years French fishermen found their way to that storehouse of finny treasures, — the Banks of Newfoundland. In 1524, the king of France, Francis the First, sent out a Florentine named Verazzano, to make a French claim in the New World, for Spain and Portugal were getting on much too fast to suit their royal neighbor. Verazzano reached a portion of the Atlantic coast which is supposed to have been what is now North Carolina. He, too, followed the coast northward, exploring some seven hundred leagues. He called the whole region New France.

When three years more had passed, an Englishman, one Thomas Thorne, was inspired to attempt the investigation of the North American coast as far as the North Pole. Henry the Eighth gave him two ships for the trip. Thorne only reached the entrance to the Gulf of Saint Lawrence, when one of the ships was cast away. The other went south again as far as Cape Breton and thence returned home.

In 1534 we see France again looking up her claims in this much-visited region, and Jacques Cartier lands in New Brunswick, where he finds the country very pleasing and the natives friendly. The next year, with greater facilities for discovery, Cartier returned and viewed the sites of the future cities, Quebec and Montreal. And once again did Cartier find his way to the country that was henceforth to be known as Canada,—a name borrowed from the little Indian village of Kannata. Elaborate preparations for founding a French colony had been made. The office of Viceroy was conferred upon Roberval, under whose

name the colony is known in history.
Cartier had charge of the fleet. He
seems to have acted quite independently,
preceding Roberval to the New World
and deserting him to return to France when it pleased himself. This colony of 1541 proved a failure, as did several others attempted.

CARTIER.

It was not until the year 1604 that an actual settlement was made in what we now call Nova Scotia.
It was then
that the truly romantic history of *Acadie*
began. The settlers came from France,
and all expected to grow rich by trading
in furs. Their leader was De Monts, who

A BIT OF ACADIAN HISTORY.

held his commission from Henry the Fourth of France — "King Henry of Navarre." They sailed about the southern and western coasts of *Acadie*, and when they entered the beautiful body of water now known as Annapolis Basin, Champlain, who had command of the vessels, named both the harbor and the river flow-

ENTRANCE TO ANNAPOLIS BASIN.

ing into it, Port Royal. No other place pleased them so well, and there they decided the following spring to build their town, which also bore the name Port Royal. And here, indeed, was the capital of Acadia until the founding of Halifax by the English in 1749.

Surely no community ever lived amid more romantic surroundings than did the colonists of Port Royal. They had many trials and deprivations in their new home in the wilderness, but they contrived various festivities to brighten their lot. Among their number were gentlemen who had been accustomed to court life, and each did his share to entertain his companions.

CHAMPLAIN.

Fifteen of the leading men organized a social club styled *The Order of the Good Time (L'Ordre de bon Temps)*. Feasting on the best that could be procured — and

fish and game were plenty—was followed by story telling, in which the Indians, who mingled picturesquely with the company, took a part. The old chief, Membertou, rich in the experiences of his hundred years, was an honored guest at the banquets.

Meanwhile the English had made a settlement in Virginia. When they learned that there were French settlers on the same coast, although eight hundred miles distant, they decided to drive them away. So three armed vessels under a piratical commander, named Argal, were sent to destroy all the forts and dwellings of the French. Strange as it may seem, even this outrage failed to enlist any aid from France; the unhappy colony of Port Royal was left to its fate: and the sole basis of English claim to this region was the Cabot discoveries of 1497 and 1498!

This claim the English continued to enforce, and James the First gave a grant of what is now Nova Scotia and New Brunswick to a Scotch favorite, Sir William Alexander, who made luckless attempts at planting a colony.

Then in 1627 a war broke out between the two home countries. Cardinal Richelieu had formed a new company which was to have a monopoly of the fur trade in "New France." An English squadron captured Port Royal and several French vessels on their way to *Acadie* with ammunition and stores. And so the conflict went on, the unfortunate Acadians always getting the worst of it. The New England Colony, feeling that there was no room on their borders for the French, strove in their usual vigorous fashion to persecute rather than to be persecuted. A doom always hung over the French attempt to possess territory in North America. Through the long years between the first settlement in 1604 to the Treaty of Paris in 1763, Acadia was a stage whereon French actors played a many-acted tragedy. For this reason Acadia and the Acadians always touch a tender chord in generous hearts. Who can refuse sympathy to the heroes of a lost cause?

The quarrels between France and England went on into the beginning of the eighteenth century. The warlike spirit of the mother countries was abroad in the colonies. Expeditions from New England brought havoc upon the Acadians in return for what was considered sufficient provocation. At last in 1710, Port Royal was captured by New England troops, and three years later peace was concluded in the Old World by the Treaty of Utrecht. Nova Scotia, Newfoundland, and Hudson Bay Territory were then ceded to Great Britain. The name of Port Royal was changed, in honor of the English queen, to Annapolis Royal. The French inhabitants of the whole region were then considered as having no right to remain unless they would take an oath of allegiance to the British Crown. Naturally they did not feel inclined to take such an oath, and of course their English victors could not feel safe with this spirit in their midst. They felt that "to the victors belong the spoils," that Acadia was theirs by right of conquest and treaty; while the early inhabitants, still hoping that their French monarch would come to their rescue, could not make up their minds to desert his cause.

Thus things went from bad to worse, and no definite agreement could be made. There is no doubt that on many occasions the French were aggressive, but the English were equally so. It is certain that they feared their intractable neighbors, and could see no way to settle matters save by resorting to extreme measures. To their aid came that stanch New England spirit which hanged women as witches, and ground Quakers to death for not taking an oath. It was a Massachusetts commander who most rigorously executed the cruel orders concerning the Acadians; and, as if to atone for his countryman's harshness toward the poor French exiles, it was a gentle-hearted New England poet who, nearly a century afterward, wrote the poem of " Evangeline," —

" A tale of love in Acadie, home of the happy."

NEAR ANNAPOLIS BASIN.

PART II.

THE ACADIA OF TO-DAY.

"*In the fisherman's cot the wheel and the loom are still busy;
Maidens still wear their Norman caps and their kirtles of
homespun,
And by the evening fire repeat Evangeline's story.*"

YARMOUTH.

CHAPTER I.

THE BORDER LAND, YARMOUTH.

To read the poem of "Evangeline" upon the very shores where its thrilling scenes were enacted, is to greatly marvel at that poetic insight which enabled Longfellow to so perfectly portray a landscape which he never saw. It is the first part of the poem only that deals with the region known as "The Land of Evangeline." The second part follows the Acadians into their places of exile, and especially concerns the fate of the lovers, Evangeline and Gabriel. The story of the expulsion and scattering is well known, but there is a continuation of the story which is not less fascinating. It shows even better than the charming hexameters of the poet how strong was the Acadian's love for his native land, and how bitter must have been his enforced separation from it.

> "Only along the shores of the mournful and misty Atlantic
> Linger a few Acadian peasants, whose fathers from exile
> Wandered back to their native land to die in its bosom."

History and existing circumstances tell us that of the three thousand exiles who were carried out of Acadia in 1755, about two thirds returned, in spite of opposition and hardships, to find new homes in such places as were not occupied by the English. Some found their perilous way back in the course of a few months, and others were weary years in reaching the home of their youth. The beautiful valley which had been for them the scene of so much horror was never to be again an Acadian settlement. Strangers soon took possession of it and shut out the old dwellers, even had they had the heart to return. It is in another part of the Acadia of to-day that we must seek the descendants of the exiles of 1755.

A pilgrim to *Nouvelle-Écosse*, the French name for Nova Scotia, has to-day the choice of many routes. If he desire, as did the pilgrim who now writes of her visit to Acadian shrines, to reach the abode of Acadian manners and customs, he can find no pleasanter way than by going direct from Boston to Yarmouth. A period of seventeen hours suffices to bring your steamer into the most opaque

YARMOUTH HARBOR.

of Fundy fogs and plant her firmly in the unsavory mud, until the tide serves to float her to the wharf. To the voyager from the West Country the grim dampness and enforced delay are trying. He longs to go ashore, to run the gantlet of the customs officers, and — have breakfast. He tells the steward of his desires, and receives the bland reply, —

"Breakfast is ready in the saloon!"

Yet who that has come up on deck, eager to land on an unknown shore, would wish to return to the stifling atmosphere "below" for breakfast?

"Thank you, but I will wait," is the somewhat stiff reply directed at the white-jacketed steward, who is already far sped on one of his many errands.

Once ashore and settled in the comfortable though not luxurious hotel, the fog ceases to annoy, and you find it quite warm enough as you walk about the Yarmouth streets, so delightful in their novelty. In the shop windows you see English goods, and are almost surprised that the prices are not marked in English money. At the house windows are great clusters of pelargoniums in lovely tints, expanding in the moist, mild air. And the hawthorn hedges! Sometimes you pass a street where house after house has its wall of green hedge, and as you look up the street, the effect is an English picture. Here and there one sees straggling growths that suggest the careless owner, but for the most part the hedges of Yarmouth are well kept and a delight to the eye.

The luminosity of the atmosphere gives one the finest effects in landscape and marine. Here for a moment the sun, pushing aside the gray curtain of fog, touches into clear outline an antique gable; there the sail of a yacht, caught by the fleeting brightness, gleams white from afar. See yonder shore as it comes into misty prominence and fades again from view — a vista from dreamland — a Fata Morgana! This is a land for poets and dreamers, for seers and idealists, this country by the Fundy Bay. Let not the realist bring hither his palette of glaring tints and his brushes of coarse fibre, for this is an Enchanted Land, and only he who bears with him the magician's lamp can see its beauties aright.

The Clare Settlements, where live the descendants of the exiles, lie a little to the north of Yarmouth. There, at a place called Meteghan, my guide-book indicated an interesting settlement and a fine French Catholic church. In the post-office at Yarmouth was a young assistant, whose liquid, dark eyes suggested French ancestry. I asked her if she came from Clare, but she said no. Then the postmaster came forward and advised me to go to

Pubnico rather than to Clare, for there, he said, lived the famous descendants of the old family of D'Entremont, in whose veins runs some of the bluest blood of France. Later research proved that Pubnico is considered the oldest Acadian settlement in

NEAR YARMOUTH.

the world, for its people returned to the same locality when their exile was ended. Pubnico, with such attractions, was hard to resist, but it lay in an opposite direction from Meteghan ; and there I had decided to spend Sunday.

DIGBY.

CHAPTER II.

BY SAINT MARY'S BAY.

(METEGHAN, CHURCH POINT.)

THE Clare Settlements are in the southwestern part of Digby County. They border on an arm of the Bay of Fundy called Saint Mary's Bay. This beautiful stretch of water was named by Champlain. At various points along its shore settled those Acadians who returned from exile. Here their descendants live quietly and speak the language of their ancestors. They retain many of the old customs, and give little thought to the outside world.

The railway from Yarmouth to Annapolis does not skirt the shore of Saint

BYWAY NEAR DIGBY.

Mary's Bay, but runs through a rather monotonous landscape. The true way to enjoy the beauties of any country is to walk or drive through its byways. This is especially true of Nova Scotian scenery, and every native will advise the tourist to drive. But this, in out-of-the-way places, is extremely difficult to do, for the few horses have their appointed daily tasks, and there are none for extra occasions. Therefore, the best that can be done is to travel by rail, tarrying at various points of interest long enough to see them satisfactorily.

The morning of my trip to Meteghan was foggy, and little could be seen from the car window. Several young women got in at way stations, and left us again, having, by their voluble remarks to one another, proved that they were Acadian French. The handsome and dignified old conductor, who looked like a Scotch doctor of divinity, seemed uncertain about hotel accommodations at Meteghan. He came to see his passenger off the train when it stopped at the modest station which seems at first glance a veritable "house in the woods." Then the train rolled away, and the passenger was left at the mercy of the few station officials and the other arrivals, all standing about and chattering French. Prominent in the group was the sole representative of the sole public house of Meteghan, into whose care the conductor had consigned the "woman who wanted to visit the French people."

The landlord was not a Frenchman, but he gave orders to his servant in very good French, collected his passengers in the same tongue, and occasionally reassured his guest in softly spoken English. At length the luggage was safely stowed into a light wagon and started on its way. The passengers were to follow in the mail coach, — for the good landlord carries her Majesty's mails, — and he was himself our driver.

There was quite a group of home-comers, sons and daughters of Meteghan, who had come from Boston for their vacation. French was the medium of conversation, and for some time the stranger listened only to the happy gossip of her companions, who were all old acquaintances glad to be together again. At length she ventured a carefully constructed remark in their language, and was met with cordial and voluble appreciation.

"*Elle parle français, elle comprend! Vous parlez français? Oui, vous parlez bien!*"

And of course they could all speak English, for they were earning their living among English-speaking people. So the conversation became general, and English or French was spoken as it happened.

It was a delightful drive of six miles to the town. As we reached the long street, our companions left us, one after another, at the pretty cottages at whose gates stood expectant friends. There was among the home-comers a rather unimpressive young fellow of some twenty years, who talked a good deal and assumed worldly ways. Two children stood at a house-door waiting for this big brother, their faces bright with expectation. As the coach approached the house, he swung himself down, without waiting for the horses to be pulled up. Rushing toward the little ones, he seized them in his arms and kissed them with the perfect abandon of affection. It was a touching Acadian tableau!

The pretty girl on the back seat continued to the hotel. She was the landlord's daughter, and before I left we had become very good friends. The family consisted of several grown-up daughters, and a son, a gentle-eyed *belle-mère*, and three small children. Not a word of unkindness nor an angry tone was to be heard. When by themselves they always spoke French.

The hotel was one of the oldest houses in Meteghan, and the landlord was preparing to remodel it and make it more suitable for a public house. He had enjoyed a monopoly of the commercial travellers and rare tourists who came his way, and being honest and unwilling to run in debt had deferred his repairs too long. All that housewifely care could do to make the superannuated rooms attractive was done. At the front of the house was an old porch with a seat built along one side — a suggestion of that in the house of Benedict Bellefontaine, —

> " Rudely carved was *the porch*, with seats beneath ";

and

> "There in the shade of *the porch* were the priest and the notary seated."

It has always been the custom in Acadian villages to build the houses along both sides of one long street. Allusion to this fact occurs in the poem, —

> " When brightly the sunset lighted *the village street*,"
>
> . . . .
>
> " Solemnly down *the street* came the parish priest,"
>
> . . . .
>
> " Down *the long street* she passed."

The street at Meteghan is lined with houses for a distance of perhaps a mile. Some are old and weather beaten, but many are trim cottages with porches and bay-windows, and pretty bits of garden in front. Sitting at the wide front window of the public sitting-room at the hotel, one could see across the way the neatest of white cottages with piazza, bay-windows, and the characteristic roof window of "the Provinces," known as the A window. In its white-fenced garden stood tall hollyhocks of rich wine color. Beyond the cottage lay the bay, obscured often during my stay by rain or mist.

The family of my host were anxious to aid me in acquiring a knowledge of Acadian manners and legends. On the first afternoon the *belle-mère* took me to visit the priest, who is much beloved by his parish. They say they owe their fine brick church to his efforts; that he freely gave of his own means to build it, had the bricks made, and induced the people to haul them with their ox-teams to the site of the church. They are proud of his energy, but fail to equal it in their own lives. The church is a tall edifice with two spires, standing upon elevated ground and facing the bay. As it is visible for miles on the sea, it has received the name *Stella Maris* — Star of the Sea. Priest and people love the edifice which is so directly the product of their own industry.

We went through one of the front gates, walking between the church and the graveyard toward the priest's dwelling in the rear. A flaxen-haired little maid and a shaggy terrier gave us a shy welcome. As the door was wide open and no one else appeared, we entered and took seats in the parlor, while the little maid went in search of "auntie," who presently came to give us welcome. After a little the good father appeared, and although he had been awakened from his after-dinner nap, was very gracious. He regretted that he could not throw much light upon early Acadian history. Although he had ministered to Acadian parishes for thirty years, he was not a Frenchman. He mentioned several French priests whom I would meet as I went on my journey. It was a little disappointment not to find an Acadian priest at Meteghan; it would have been more in harmony with people and place, and — *more like the poem.* Still these people love their priest even as those at Grand Pré loved the good Father Felician. He speaks their language well, and they seem to know no difference.

Later in the day the gentle Adèle took me to visit the oldest woman in the village, one Madame Thibedeau. She was a dignified and amiable old lady, very proud of being the great-granddaughter of an Acadian exile. Her maiden name was *Doucette*, — a name which figures in the annals of *Acadie*. Pierre Doucette, the exile, had been

A NOVA SCOTIA COTTAGE.

a resident of Port Royal prior to the expulsion, and was transported by the English to the vicinity of Casco Bay. With his companions he made his way back to the shores of *Baie Sainte-Marie*.

The little house where madame and her husband live was the picture of neatness.

The floors and stairs were painted yellow, as, indeed, they often are in Acadian cottages. At the windows were pretty blooming house plants, — one a sweet-scented, old-fashioned "monthly rose." None of this family could speak English. They had preserved their language as well as their traditions.

On Sunday morning I attended mass with my host and his household. In the church a stranger always gets his best impressions of a community. A good many women and some young girls in the congregation wore the *couvre-chef* in place of bonnet or hat. This is a black kerchief of wool or silk, worn in three-corner fashion and tied under the chin. The dress was also black. On several occasions I saw one of these black-robed figures in the little churchyard, kneeling before a grave offering prayers for the dead. So much that one sees in the *Acadie* of to-day suggests the poem of "Evangeline."

> "Without in the churchyard
> Waited the women. They stood by the graves and hung on the headstones
> Garlands of autumn leaves and evergreens fresh from the forest."

The graveyard was a tangle of wild

roses and other rank-growing wild things, running all about the simple monuments to those who sleep below. Perhaps these wild blossoms pay tribute to the dead, and rise like truth from the dust of those who did their best to love their neighbors and serve their God.

The interior of Stella Maris is rather too bare and new to be attractive to the eye. The three altars are decorated in the usual elaborate fashion. Most fitting amid the display seemed the beautiful natural plants; these always speak of their Maker, and awaken

"Thoughts that do often lie too deep for tears."

The priest in his fine robes was imposing, and the altar boys in their red and white were very devout in their many duties. At the close of the service the priest came forward and made a short address in French. He told his hearers not to forget that the next day would be the Fête of the Holy Virgin, or Assumption of the Virgin. He besought them to return with fervor their thanks for the prosperity of the past year. This day, the fifteenth of August, is annually celebrated by the Acadians, who feel that heaven has especially favored them in bringing them back from exile and permitting them to grow as a people. The day itself is marked by religious services, and the two following days are given up to festivities. The people gather from all parts and meet for a general good time at the "convention," as it is called.

Monday morning as I walked through the street, enjoying the long perspective of pretty cottages, a young woman at a doorway shyly invited me to enter. I accepted gladly, for there is always a great charm about interiors. This cottage was very tasty. There were several pictures on the wall of the little parlor, mostly in the line of religious art. One was quite novel. It represented a group engaged in the marriage ceremony at the altar. Below were signed the names of the contracting parties and the witnesses. My hostess could not speak English, but we got on very pleasantly. She took me into the family room to see an oleander in bloom. Here was a very pretty *buffet* with glass doors, built into the wall. Within were arranged the glassware and pretty blue china. The tiny garden before the house held a riot of small flowers and the darkest hollyhocks I ever saw, almost *black*. The French people must be very fond of this *Passe-Rose*, as they call it.

At intervals during the day people wended their way to the church services. A good many boys and men appeared to have too much time on their hands, and loitered about the street and doorsteps. There was plenty of work about the houses and barns, for the outside of the Acadian home is far less tidy than the inside. It is evidently the women who are thrifty and industrious. All the houses have patchwork quilts and carefully arranged sets of curtains. No window has less than two kinds. On the floors are many rugs, some really artistic in their construction, and all of them the product of skill and hard work. Before one of the church altars is a beautiful rug in raised work, designed and made by the young girl whose gift it was. In addition to all these proofs of feminine industry are the sewing and cooking, washing and ironing, for the always large family. Meteghan is a fishing community, as are most of the villages on Saint Mary's Bay, so we may not expect to see the well-tilled farms of the rich dike country where the early Acadians lived.

If, however, the men and boys would follow the good example of their wives and sisters, there would be a great change for the better about the houses of Clare. Within they are orderly and attractive, but without they often show want of care.

On Monday afternoon I went with Adèle to visit the convent where she used to attend school. A gravelled walk led up to the front entrance. In the square vestibule were pretty house plants. Through the quiet, cool hall came, in response to our ring, a *petite* sister, whose dark eyes and little black glazed bonnet made her look very pale. She gave us a cordial greeting, and showed us about the convent. The pupils were all away for the summer vacation. Everything in the house was simple, almost to austereness, but the chapel was daintily pretty. The room was all in white. The tiny altar, draped in white, was adorned with flowers. At one side stood a white-draped image of the Virgin, at the feet the sacred fire, burning under a small shade of soft red glass.

The next morning the fog which had been haunting the bay, and often enveloped the whole community, had gone.

Blue sky and bluer water made the world seem new again. I started early for Church Point, the scene of the Acadian gathering or "convention." The station, like most in this region, is several miles from the settlement, and is in this case only a rough shed. A girl, who got in at Meteghan, and I were the only women to alight. There was no public conveyance to be seen, but the driver of a single-seated wagon came forward and offered to convey us to the scene of festivity. Away we bounced over sand bars and close to puddles, the mud flying high, and the fresh breeze nearly taking our breath. As we approached the town our driver became more decorous in his management of the reins. Soon a peal of welcome sounded from the church, which now appeared to our left. It was a welcome to the Superior of the *Collège Sainte-Anne*, who was coming close behind us. We looked back and saw several priests in a carriage drawn by a fine span of horses. Our driver drew his horse aside to let them pass us. The Superior was returning from a visit to France, his native land, and added to the general happiness by his return just at this time.

Church and college were decorated with streamers of bunting, and presented a gala appearance. Our driver dropped us with apparent relief outside the grounds where the festivities were going on, and pocketing his fee, left us to make our way. The girl was very kind, and assisted me to find a lady whose acquaintance I had made at Meteghan, and who had promised to show me how to enjoy the "convention." And well she kept her word! A direct descendant of the exiles, she recounted with ready fidelity such bits of their story as were known to her, and presented me to others who could add their information. Her great-grandmother, born at Salem, Massachusetts, was the child of exiles named Surette. Like Evangeline and Gabriel, these married lovers were taken to separate ships, but never met each other again on earth. The mother and her posthumous daughter came back in course of time to *Acadie*, but the hope of their hearts was not fulfilled; the child was never to know her father, the wife never to hear again the voice of her beloved.

"Far asunder, on separate coasts, the Acadians landed;
  Scattered were they, like flakes of snow, when the wind from
    the northeast

Strikes aslant through the fogs that darken the Banks of
Newfoundland.
. . . .
Friends they sought and homes; and many despairing, heart-
broken,
Asked of the earth but a grave, and no longer a friend nor a
fireside."

At Church Point, on Saint Mary's Bay,
the first church erected by the returned
Acadian exiles is said to have stood. For
more than thirty years after their return
the people had neither priest nor house of
worship. But in July, 1799, there came to
them exactly the man who was demanded
by the peculiar condition of Acadian affairs. In the words of his recent eulogist,*
the Abbé Sigogne was "an enlightened
apostle filled with zeal; a wise governor,
faithful to the British government, and
honored by its confidence; a charitable
shepherd devoted to his flock."

L'Abbé Jean-Mandé Sigogne was born
at Tours in 1760, and was ordained to the
priesthood in 1785. Refusing to swear
allegiance to the Constitution during the
dreadful days of the French Revolution,
he was condemned to the guillotine. On
the day appointed for his death he made
his escape into England. There he em-

---
* R. Ph. F. Bourgeois, Professor at Collège Sainte-Anne.

ployed himself in teaching French, Latin, and Greek. Having been persecuted himself, he resolved to devote his life to those who had also suffered injustice, especially to the church, for whose sake he had already risked so much. Eight days after his arrival at Halifax, the English capital of Nova Scotia, he took the oath of allegiance to the British Crown. He taught his people fidelity to the government under whose protection they found themselves, and to this union was due the great temporal success which attended the hitherto disheartened and misjudged Acadians. For forty-five years the Abbé Sigogne labored among the descendants of the exiles of 1755 and the neighboring Indians. During twenty-one years he was the sole missionary in charge of a territory one hundred and thirty miles in extent. In the autumn of 1844, the aged priest was stricken with paralysis while conducting a service at the altar. Three days later he died, beloved and mourned by those whose benefactor he had so long and devotedly been.

On the 19th of May, 1892, his honored remains were removed from the church where he had been interred and placed under a green mound in front of the College of Saint Anne. A white marble monument, with appropriate inscriptions, crowns the mound; and thither will go many pilgrims as the years roll on.

The College of Saint Anne has but recently been erected. It is a fine large edifice with modern improvements, and accommodates about a hundred boys. It was incorporated by Act of the Provincial Parliament in 1892, and has power to confer degrees. Saint Anne's was established by priests from France, fathers of the Congregation of Jesus and Mary. These fathers are known as *Eudistes*, from the founder of their order, Saint Eude. They are bright, cultivated men, none of them old in appearance. They speak their own language almost exclusively, and are most genial in their manners.

One of them took a small party of us about the college. He was the most youthful of the priestly professors, a mere boy in appearance. A broad-shouldered figure, a little above medium height, an olive skin, and gray eyes shading into black, a mouth where sweetness mingled with firmness, — these made up the exterior of such a son as might gladden any mother's heart. Truth and honesty, with a dash of boyish good-nature, looked out of the face of the young "Father" as he was called by courtesy, for he was not yet old enough to be admitted to the priesthood. And the black *soutane* was so well put on, and hung so proudly from the strong, young shoulders; the knotted black sash fell so boyishly at his side, and the low beaver hat, with its broad rim caught up against the crown, was so bewitching when on, and so deferential when doffed and carried in the slim, brown hand! He spoke no English, but the purest French came musically to our ears as he chatted of the college and his work. In the music-room we listened with delight as he sang a French *chanson*. He is a poet, too, this youthful Eudiste, and composed a beautiful processional hymn for the Corpus Christi *fête*, which was celebrated on the 16th of June.

The college grounds are not far from the shore of the bay, and a path winds down to the lighthouse, gleaming in the sun on the day that I was at Church Point. Along this path the procession took its way, the young girls of the vicinity all in white, and bearing flowers in their hands. At the end of the path, near the ruins of the first church, and at two intervening points, were erected small bowers of spruce boughs called "Repositories." At these the procession halted while a priest celebrated a mass; at the last one the *Benediction* was said. As my Acadian friend and I went on that August afternoon to visit the "Repositories," the dead branches of spruce gave out a spicy fragrance that mingled with the sunlit air, like incense from an altar. Seen from a distance the effect of these arches of reddish brown spruce, each bearing at its summit a cross, was very picturesque.

Returning from our walk, a brief visit was made at the convent, which is also a school for girls, like the one at Meteghan. Here a sister entertained us, assisted by two dear little girls, who had just come from Canada to attend school. They were the first arrivals for the new term, and seemed too young to be sent away from home care. But the sisters are sweet and kind, and make their young charges very happy. Here, again, the chapel was fitted up with a white altar and flowers.

In a small house at the other side of the college live several sisters of the Eudiste Order. Four of them had recently come from France, and it was easy to fancy them as being a little homesick. They keep in order the linen of the college, and do other domestic work. The Superior conversed very cheerfully with my companions. She and a little Acadian novice were the only ones at home. The head-gear of this order is quite elaborate. A stiff white muslin band crosses the forehead and turns away from the cheeks with an Egyptian effect. The stiff bow under the chin is also white. Over the head from the white band on the forehead is gathered a black veil. From this effective frame the cheerful face of the Superior, lighted by its dark, sparkling eyes, looked out. The novice, a pretty maid, wore under the ordinary black bonnet a little white cap.

The festivities in the college grounds went on all day, with no apparent weariness on the part of the participants. In the refectory long tables had been spread by the women of the parish, and loaded with the things that constitute a substantial cold dinner. Everything was in profusion, and every one seemed bent on eating to the full extent of the twenty-five cents paid for his dinner ticket. Meats, vegetables, and bread, of many varieties; pickles, cakes, of all sizes and hues, some with gay candies on top; pies, cheese, tea and coffee, — all disappeared only to see the empty dishes replenished from the unfailing stores brought by the Acadian housewives. Square wooden chests stood behind the tables against the wall, ready to yield more good things as the demands were made.

My kind Acadian friend made arrangements for me to remain over night at the house of some of her relatives. Here I found myself on veritable historic ground. The house, quite new and roomy, was erected on the site of an older one. Just outside the parlor windows stood those ruined reminders of the early French settlers, for which I had learned to scan every landscape, gnarled and scrubby apple-trees and willows. These grew, or rather survived, upon the edge of the otherwise obliterated garden. A few struggling garden shrubs had outlived the desolation, and rose apologetically here and there from the rank, matted grass. The willows were wrecks, — with gaunt, hollow trunks, but with a toppling mass of foliage, fed apparently on rich memories of the past. The mistress of the modern house has a brood of young children, and finds no time to renovate old gardens.

The first house built at Church Point by the returned exiles stood on these grounds at some little distance from the present one and nearer the bay. In the evening three of us set out to find the cellar and well which our host said were just discernible, provided we knew the exact place to look for them. We wandered on through the long, thick grass, but could not find the depressions for which we sought. Instead, we found the great ridge of pebbles thrown up by "the turbulent tides" of Saint Mary's Bay, so high that it quite cut off our view of the shore and the water on the other side. We clambered to the summit and beheld the bay at our feet. Across the water, ruffled only by the evening breeze, lay the long tongue of land that separates Saint Mary's from the Fundy Bay. This land is Digby Neck, — a portion of the main peninsula of Nova Scotia. At its southern extremity lies Long Island, and between the two is the strait retaining its French name, *Petit Passage.* Another island, the last barrier point between the bays, is separated from Long Island by *Grand Passage.* Its name is Bryer Island.

The tide was going, and we strolled upon the beach. My companions pointed out the spot where their exiled ancestors, returning from Massachusetts, had found a haven for their little vessel while they viewed the land. How real it all seemed as we stood in the evening light, under the same sky and gazed upon the same landscape, the same but less desolate now than then! To our right the starry lantern of the lighthouse sent forth its com-

LIGHTHOUSE, SAINT MARY'S BAY.

forting beams. Across the bay were lights that betokened dwellers on the narrow strand, and at the left the hamlet of Port Acadie caught the glory of the sun that slowly sank to rest. As we turned and reached the top of the drift, lights were appearing in the windows of the college, which was to be illuminated during the evening. A grand concert and fireworks were also on the programme. The Acadians were indefatigable in their enjoyment, but I decided to view these late festivities from afar. It was a beautiful August night. The western sky long retained the glow of twilight, paling from orange to amber ere it changed to dusk. The summer constellations sparkled on high. Then in puny imitation of their splendor shot up from the college grounds a cluster of Roman candles or a more aspiring skyrocket. It was the first pyrotechnic display that this region had ever beheld, and cheers of approbation resounded through the quiet night.

The following morning our host took us to the real site of the first house at Church Point. It was not easy to find it unless one knew where it was, for the depressions are filled up nearly level with the surrounding field, and only a few building stones mark the corners of the place where the old cellar used to be. "There was a forest all about at the time they landed," said our host in French. "They could easily get timber for their houses. And there was

RAILWAY BRIDGE AT BEAR RIVER.

fish in the bay, so it was a good place here," he continued. "The women carried stones for the cellar walls in their aprons."

The good time was to be prolonged for another day. As I sat upon the doorstep waiting for a team to take me to the station, I could see groups of Acadians proceeding along the highway that led to the college and picnic grounds. Gayly dressed girls with bright parasols went by, seated in slow-moving ox-carts.

"Now from the country around, from the farms and neighboring hamlets,
Came in their holiday dresses the blithe Acadian peasants.
Many a glad good-morrow and jocund laugh from the young folk
Made the bright air brighter, as up from the numerous meadows,
Where no path could be seen but the track of wheels in the greensward,
Group after group appeared, and joined, or passed on the highway."

Another living picture from the poem!

"This will be the best day of all," said my Acadian friend. "To-day they have potato soup (*soupe à la patate*) for sale on the grounds. Could you not stay and try some of it? They will make a lot of money to-day."

" I could stay forever with *les Acadiens*," I replied; "but I must away to other scenes

— to the Annapolis Valley and the real 'Land of Evangeline'; but here are the spirit and the race of that lovely Acadian maid. All other places will be

> 'Incomplete, imperfect, unfinished,'

for in them all

> ' Dwells another race, with other customs and language.' "

Since the day when the Acadians were driven from their homes, the places that once knew them have known them no more. A few years after their removal large numbers of New England colonists came and took possession of the rich meadows that had been the fertile farms of the unhappy exiles.

PART III.

OLD ACADIAN HAUNTS.

"*Louisburg is not forgotten, nor Beau Séjour nor Port Royal.*"

ON THE WAY TO ANNAPOLIS.

CHAPTER I.

ANNAPOLIS ROYAL.

(OLD PORT ROYAL OF THE FRENCH.)

THE journey from Church Point to Annapolis is made beautiful by glimpses of Saint Mary's Bay and Annapolis Basin. Several fine bridges are crossed by the railway, — bridges that for height and length of span are thrilling enough if the passenger ventures to put his head outside the car window and look down and back. As we approach the junction of the Annapolis River with the basin, our longing eyes are rewarded by the first glimpse of real *dikes.* Although of a very unimposing type, they make us feel that we are now come into "the Acadian land" of the poem. Now will we

" List to the mournful tradition,"

which ocean, forest, and "murmuring pines" relate to sympathizing ears.

Annapolis Royal, as its more aristocratic residents still write it when they date their letters, has little to show of Acadian memories outside its old French graveyard and its old French fort. My landlady having informed me that a funeral was to take place in the graveyard, which was directly across the street, I went over in due season. The oldest tombstones are said to have been of perishable material, and I found none with an earlier date than 1743. The sexton, who hovered about in nervous expectation of the burial train, assured me that there was one very much older, but he was not able to find it. Neither was he able or desirous to prevent a quartet of *gamins,* one of whom was a darky, from playing various pranks about the edge of

EVENING SHADOWS IN THE ACADIAN LAND.

the newly opened grave. He invited me to inspect some bones that lay mouldering at the bottom of the grave, and turned them over with a stick for my better view.

"They must have belonged to a French soldier," was his conclusion. "And he was a very big man too, for that's a long bone," he said, as he scratched a little earth over it.

The grave had been opened for an aged lady who was descended from one of the old French families. Shortly after the procession entered the gate of the cemetery, the clergyman in his robes, preceding the coffin, reading the solemn words of the burial service.

The moat which surrounded the old fort probably enclosed also the adjoining burying ground and may still be traced along one side. Near one end is a group of ancient willows. One late wild rose, growing on a straggling bush on the summit of the uneven terrace that marks the moat, seemed waiting to be plucked and carried away,—a sweet reminder of the dreamy old spot.

The fort grounds impress one by their extent,—some twenty-eight acres. They lie in the very heart of the town, and are a most delightful pleasure-ground. There are many picturesque points in the vicinity, and the views of water and hills to be had from the ramparts are well worth seeing. The mind travels involuntarily to the early settlers, and wonders how the region looked to them as they came upon it before the foot of any white man had touched its green shores, — beautiful but yet a wilder-

FRAGMENT OF OLD FRENCH FORT AT ANNAPOLIS.

ness. Over the grassy outlines of moat and rampart cattle now browse contentedly.

All that remains of French masonry is the crumbling sally-port and the small but solid powder magazine. The interior of this little structure is damp and dimly lighted. Its walls are built of blocks of

SCENERY NEAR ANNAPOLIS.

limestone, known as Caen stone, brought long ago from France. Dampness and age have worn the stone so soft that one may easily mark it with one's finger nail and in some places it may be scraped off like salt. The stone was originally of a creamy white, but has taken on tints of green and brown, so that, as one enters, the effect is most pleasing. No effort has been made by government to keep these historical relics in a state of preservation. The matter has been agitated, but should have been thoroughly attended to long since. The quaint, long building with broad chimneys, now occupied by tenants of the poorer class, was the British barracks. The old French barracks became unsafe and were taken down some years ago.

The general air of Annapolis at the present day is English; very little except the natural scenery reminds us of the Acadians. Relics have been dug up and certain rare, archæologically inclined residents are familiar with the old haunts of the French people, who really gave its historic and poetic charm to their serious, little British town.

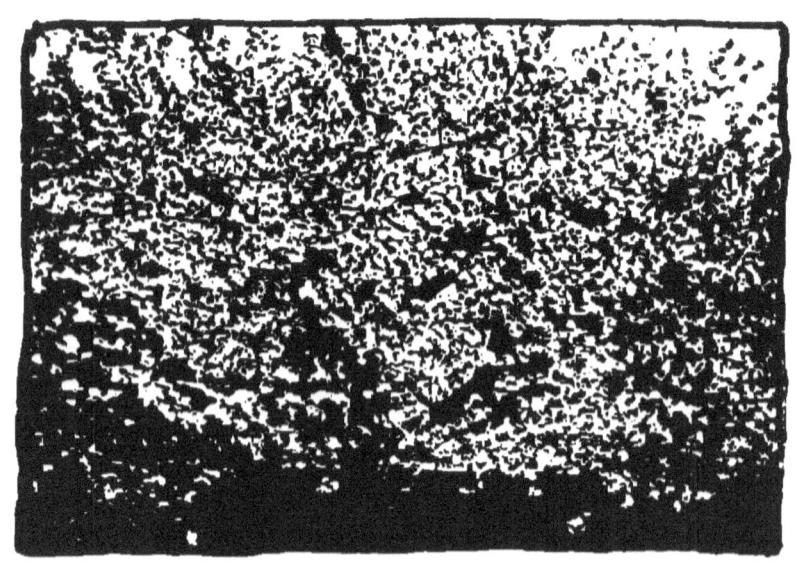

APPLE BLOSSOMS, ANNAPOLIS VALLEY.

CHAPTER II.

IN THE ANNAPOLIS VALLEY.

SOME twelve miles up the valley from Annapolis I found a delightful abiding-place from which to study the scenic handling of the poem. Here at a farmhouse on the side of the South Mountain I tarried, under the spell of the landscape. For over a fortnight, during which I walked and drove with great frequency, I revelled in the beauties of the Annapolis Valley.

The valley is wide enough to give the right stretch of foreground as one looks across the river from either mountain-side. The mountains are covered with verdure, and are fascinating in sunlight and in fog. Indeed, the fog effects upon the North Mountain are enchanting. Often and often I stood in the doorway of the old house, and looked with rapture where —

"Sea-fogs pitched their tents, and mists from the mighty Atlantic
Looked on the happy valley, but ne'er from their station descended."

Driven in from the Bay of Fundy, the great wall of mist shuts out for a time the entire upper outline of the mountain. Then by some mysterious process it is caught up like great rolls of wool and lies along the summit, never coming down into the valley. One may look at intervals for hours, and always find some change has taken place. And then as sunset time approaches, the last thin trails disappear, and the glory of purple and gold touches the hilltop into clear outline, growing darker as the sky grows brighter.

The river, too, is subject to changes that make it interesting to the visitor. Affected by the Fundy tides, it rises higher than an ordinary river, and is consequently very curious to see at low tide. Then the narrow, shallow waterway lies at the bottom of a shelving trough of shimmering red-brown mud, rising many times the water's width above it. All along the river banks stretch the dikes that protect the marshes from the rushing tides, which would carry away their richness. One may see, too, some of those curious constructions used for flooding the marshes when necessary. These are still called by their Acadian name, — *aboteaux*. They were made by binding together stout spruce trees, and served as a kind of sluiceway.

"At stated seasons the flood gates
Opened and welcomed the sea to wander at will o'er the meadows."

The first French settlers of the valley came from a part of France where the sea was kept out by artificial dikes, and were, therefore, able to manage the condition of things which they found in the New World. After the expulsion, the dikes and other improvements of the Acadians fell into decay, and when the English and New England settlers came to take possession it was necessary to build new dikes and to repair the old ones. For these purposes they were obliged to employ some of the Acadians still to be found in the country, as they understood the work so thoroughly. The old French dikes still in existence are pointed out to the visitor who desires to see "everything that belonged to the French."

The cellars of French houses, which some of the older people remember to have seen quite clearly defined, have now become obliterated, and one may only be shown the field where they used to be. One of the ancient wells I saw, and learned that it had been cleared out a few years before, when the original stone wall was found in good condition nearly up to the top. This was repaired, and the old spring again fills the well with good water, which is used by several families in the vicinity. It was a pretty bit of picturesqueness, just on the slope of a slight rise of ground. The grasses and vines looked over its edge at their own reflection in the water, and above all a half-dead apple-tree suggested Acadian days.

"Farther down, on the slope of the hill, was the well with its moss-grown
Bucket, fastened with iron."

At some distance back on the farm where I was staying there was a cave, in which many years ago had been found articles that had belonged to some of the fugitive Acadians, who sought safety in flight. Such relics were not unfrequently met with.

"Many already have fled to the forest, and lurk on its outskirts,
Waiting with anxious hearts the dubious fate of the morrow."

In one of my evening drives, — for the mystery and beauty of the valley are enhanced by the night, — I saw the living duplicate of this picture from the poem.

"Late with the rising moon, returned the wains from the marshes,
Laden with briny hay, that filled the air with its odor."

And again, when the moon was late, we saw the lights moving about on the marshes, and heard the farmers as they shouted to their oxen, and the creaking of the wagons as they took up their slow journey to the waiting barns.

Once, when the

"Twilight descending
Brought back the evening star to the sky,"

I walked alone to Bloody Creek, crossed the crazy bridge, and followed the uphill road that seemed to run away to the red-gold sky. At my left an orchard, fringing the sloping hill, made a picture, the dark trunks and heavy tops of the trees outlined on the sky. To the right lay stretches of fertile meadow, through which the creek winds its way to join the river. Beyond

APPLE ORCHARD, ANNAPOLIS VALLEY.

rose North Mountain, growing massive in the waning light. But few houses were in view, and I met few people on my way. As the glow of the sunset faded, I turned and came down again toward the creek, where the shadows had already gathered. It was eerie enough, but I stood for a while on the bridge listening to the ripple of the water. Away up the South Mountain, whither I had been in the afternoon, I could hear the softened rush of the falls. Close by one end of the bridge stood the aged wreck of an apple-tree, said to mark the spot where those who fell in the long-ago fight were buried. In 1711, a battle took place on the banks of the creek. So many fell that the waters ran red with blood, and its name has ever since been a reminder of the scene of carnage. The English at that time held the fort at Annapolis, and were met here by the French and their Indian allies.

One more evening reminiscence of the Annapolis Valley and I have done. The willows are said to have at least sprung from those planted by the French, and, believing this, every single tree or clump of trees gives untold satisfaction to one who has learned to love the least trace of the romantic first settlers. And when one sees, here and there, the weird Lombardy poplars that are so frequently met with in journeying through the—

"Sunny land of France,"

then is there no doubt in one's mind that here in truth was the abode of the "simple

Acadian farmers" who "dwelt together in love." So in the gloaming of a rainy day, with the fog striving to make way for the stars, we set out to visit a row of willows that were considered reliably "Acadian." Their great trunks had been pollarded, and during long subsequent years had borne a thicket of wood and foliage. They were satisfactory relics, and the homeward walk was a series of visions of beauty. We walked upon the railway, and from its elevation could overlook the winding river and the dike lands, with their harmonious tints of green. The fog was thick toward the east or up the river. The wind tore it loose from the ever-present wall of the North Mountain, and strove to drive it to the bay. Here and there the light broke through it and illumined the landscape. Then in a brief moment the rift was closed and the light shut off. The water was placid, and mirrored each object near the bank, most conspicuously the beautiful trees,—the dark green spruces and silver masses of willows, the stately elms and grotesque apple-trees.

Aground in the shallow river lay a schooner, her sails all down, the bare spars looming in the fantastic light. So might have looked one of those prison transports that lay in wait for the sorrowing exiles of 1755.

"AGROUND IN THE SHALLOW RIVER LAY A SCHOONER."

PART IV.

THE POET'S ACADIA.

(*Scene of the poem of "Evangeline."*)

"*Where is the thatch-roofed village, the home of Acadian farmers?*

. . . .

Waste are those pleasant farms, and the farmers forever departed!

. . . .

Naught but tradition remains of the beautiful village of Grand Pré."

ORCHARD IN BLOOM.

CHAPTER I.

THE CORNWALLIS VALLEY.

THE scenes depicted by Longfellow are located near the Cornwallis Valley, some seventy miles from Annapolis, and at the other end of that stretch of land which extends from Annapolis Basin on the west to the Basin of Minas on the east. The work of evicting the Acadian population was conducted simultaneously in four different places by four different military commanders acting under the governor's orders. Lieutenant-Colonel John Winslow of Massachusetts had charge of the work at Grand Pré and vicinity. His management was more successful than that of his colleagues. Although he resorted to strategy and did his cruel task so skilfully, history credits him with having said of the wretched victims of his skill, "It hurts me to hear their weeping and wailing." Let us hope it *hurt* him enough to cause due repentance for his readiness to obey the cruel orders of his superiors.

The whole Cornwallis Valley is noted for its beauty and its agricultural wealth.

APPLE PICKING.

It is often called the "Garden of Nova Scotia," and with the Annapolis Valley forms one of the greatest fruit-growing regions in the world. It was the French who first in-

THE CORNWALLIS VALLEY. 81

troduced apple culture into the Annapolis Valley about the year 1633. The shelter of the two mountain ranges, the oft-quoted North and South Mountain, makes both valleys particularly favorable for the spreading orchards that so astonish a stranger. In the time of apple blossoms, the beauty of the scene can hardly be

WOLFVILLE, NOT FAR FROM GRAND PRÉ.

imagined. And when the ripening fruit glows in the sun of late summer and early autumn, then is it a rich delight to breathe

"The odorous air of the orchard."

Scattered along the railway that passes through the Cornwallis Valley are many pretty towns. Foremost of all, to the eager pilgrim who seeks Acadian shrines, is Grand Pré. If, however, one wishes to take the many delightful outings that may be enjoyed in the vicinity, it is better to locate where one may be sure of a comfortable hotel and the privileges of a livery stable, and also see as much as possible of the life of the people. For all these purposes I found the charming little town of Kentville most admirable.

Kentville has about it a very English flavor that makes it seem quite foreign. Here are settled a considerable number of retired British officers, and the tone of its society is decidedly aristocratic. The principal streets are lively all day and until late at night. On the first morning of my sojourn, I found that something unusual was going forward, and as I walked about saw here and there a soldier. Coming in sight of the parade, there was quite a gathering of citizens, driving-parties and pedestrians, all watching with interest the movements of the young dragoons, who were mounting and falling into place with an air of great importance. They were going into camp at the Nova Scotian "Aldershot," some miles distant, and made

MINAS BASIN—BLOMIDON IN THE DISTANCE.

THE CORNWALLIS VALLEY. 85

a pleasing feature in a stranger's view of the place.

One of the pleasant trips that may be taken from Kentville is that over the Cornwallis Valley Railway to Kingsport. Kingsport is at the terminus of this short line,— only fifteen miles in length,— and is on the very edge of the Basin of Minas. Every native will say, "Oh, don't go to Kingsport; get off at Canning and see the 'Look Off.' That's a view worth having; it's a panorama of the whole country for miles around." But panoramas, however attractive to the general sight-seer, have little to offer in the way of sentiment; and the hours that were spent on the shore at Kingsport were fraught with quiet delight.

It was a clear September morning, and as I walked from the toylike car of the narrow-gauge road toward the maritime settlement of Kingsport, —

"Pleasantly gleamed in the soft, sweet air the Basin of Minas."

The sunlight danced upon the blue waves, and overhead the blue sky was sprinkled with fleecy clouds. The long pier, with its squat little lighthouse, the low-lying green meadows, with their haystacks partly swamped by the high tide, indicated the proximity of the Fundy Bay. No dikes were in sight, the village being given over to commercial interests rather than to farming. A vessel lay on the stocks, and

"A VESSEL LAY ON THE STOCKS."

the sound of hammers could be heard. The wide entrance to a smithy faced the upper end of the pier, and showed the glowing fire and the figures hovering about it. I half expected to see some modern Gabriel and his little mate looking into the fascinating place as in the poem: —

"When the hymn was sung and the daily lessons completed,
Swiftly they hurried away to the forge of Basil the blacksmith.
There at the door they stood, with wondering eyes to behold him
Take in his leathern lap the hoof of the horse as a plaything,
Nailing the shoe in its place; while near him the tire of the cart-wheel
Lay like a fiery snake, coiled round in a circle of cinders."

All along the nearer shore ran the high bluff of red clay so characteristic of the region. The white sails of a passing schooner making her outward way to the mouth of the basin caught the morning breeze as she sped onward like a thing of life. From the beach I picked some bits of rock, such as are found at Blomidon, — a grayish volcanic mass, with clusters of tiny crystals scattered through. The crystals are colored to a dull pink by the iron that tinges everything about the shore. Near the pier grew a stunted bush of willow and a coarse seashore variety of goldenrod.

As I walked along the freight railway that runs from the end of the pier to the station where I was to take the train for Kentville, I saw the full extent of the village, — its homes, its churches, and its stores. A few willows and one gaunt Lombardy caught my eye. Perchance here too had been the homes of —

"Men whose lives glided on like rivers that water the woodlands,
Darkened by shadows of earth, but reflecting an image of heaven."

CUTTING THROUGH AN ORCHARD.

CHAPTER II.

GRAND PRÉ.

"In the Acadian land on the shores of the Basin of Minas,
Distant, secluded, still, the little village of Grand Pré
Lay in the fruitful valley. Vast meadows stretched to the
  eastward,
Giving the village its name, and pasture to flocks without
  number."

FROM Kentville one may take the trip to Grand Pré by rail, or, which is more

THE GASPEREAU VALLEY.

delightful, drive through the lovely Gaspereau Valley. A pause should be made as one reaches the top of the hill at one side of the valley. He will behold a pleasing picture. The scenery is not grand in any of this region, but has a quiet beauty, and enough variety to be most attractive to the eye. Through the valley flows the little Gaspereau River, at whose mouth lay the English ships, whose appearance there brought so much anxiety to Basil, the blacksmith of Grand Pré: —

> "Four days now are passed since the English ships at their anchors
> Ride in the Gaspereau's mouth, with their cannon pointed against us.
> What their design may be is unknown; but all are commanded
> On the morrow to meet in the church, where his Majesty's mandate
> Will be proclaimed as law in the land. Alas! in the mean time
> Many surmises of evil alarm the hearts of the people."

As we entered the village of Grand Pré we drove up before the house of a man who, my driver said, would show us some relics that had been dug up in the neighborhood. This he did, but with the manner of one who wondered why anybody should desire to see such things. The relics are undoubtedly reliable. They all show the effects of lying long hidden in the damp earth. Their present owner

4

makes quizzical remarks as he carelessly hands them to his visitor. The long, rusty key, he says, was the key of the chapel where the French people were shut up by the soldiers. It may have been so. A great cow-bell, worn into holes by the moisture of the earth, belonged, so says

OLD BLACKSMITH FORGE, GRAND PRÉ.

this exhibitor of Acadian relics, to Evangeline's heifer. With this statement he gives a sly wink to my driver, and seems to be highly pleased with his own ingenuity. But what matters a little scoffing on the part of those who have no sympathy with the traditions of Grand Pré? Has not the poet given us this picture, and does it not rise before us as we take the clumsy bell into our hands?

> "Foremost, bearing the bell, Evangeline's beautiful heifer,
> Proud of her snow-white hide, and the ribbon that waved from
>   her collar,
> Quietly paced and slow, as if conscious of human affection."

And then, tempted by our evident credulity, the showman points to a blacksmith's shop a few yards away, and declares with mischief in his eyes that it is Basil's.

As we drove on over the long, white road leading to the railway, and the supposed site of the Acadian village of Grand Pré, there was a fine view of the Basin of Minas and the dikes.

> "And away to the northward Blomidon rose."

Cape Blomidon is the great headland that forms the terminus of the North Mountain range. It is a grand feature in the scenery, jutting out boldly into the basin. Geologically, it is of great interest. Almost every visitor who is persevering brings away pretty mineral specimens. The bulk of the bluff is red sandstone. Agates, chalcedony, amethysts, and variously tinted quartz crystals are found. Indian legends made Blomidon the residence of the great deity Glooscap. Here

he held his court and kept the wild animals under control. At the coming of the white man, he left the region in a great rage, having first performed various miraculous deeds. He it was who scattered the gems about Blomidon. Some

"AWAY TO THE NORTHWARD BLOMIDON ROSE."

day, so the legends tell, he will come again to the scene of his former power.

Willows and Lombardy poplars abound at Grand Pré. We passed one fine old mansion that might well have been the home of —

"Benedict Bellefontaine, the wealthiest farmer of Grand Pré";

for it seemed to answer the description : —

> "Firmly builded with rafters of oak, the house of the farmer
> Stood on the side of a hill commanding the sea;
> . . . . .
> and a footpath
> Led through an orchard wide, and disappeared in the meadow."

Not far from the station is the clump of willows believed to mark the site of the church where the unsuspecting men and boys of the village were decoyed on that sad September day of 1755. It is very easy to conjure up a picture of the tragic scene.

> "With a summons sonorous
> Sounded the bell from its tower, and over the meadows a drum beat.
> Thronged erelong was the church with men.
> . . . . .
> Then came the guard from the ships, and marching proudly among them
> Entered the sacred portal. With loud and dissonant clangor
> Echoed the sound of their brazen drums from ceiling and casement,—
> Echoed a moment only, and slowly the ponderous portal
> Closed, and in silence the crowd awaited the will of the soldiers."

Close by the church was the priest's house, now marked by the ancient well, which has been restored and is protected by a white railing. The destruction of Grand Pré was so thoroughly accomplished that it has always been difficult to locate the places of interest. The Connecticut colonists, who came to live here about five years after the expulsion, found some farming implements and the bones of many cattle that had perished by hunger and exposure. A few families were

OLD ACADIAN GRAVEYARD, GASPEREAU.

found, living like savages in the woods, where they had fled to avoid the soldiers. From time to time relics have continued to be discovered, — tools, fragments of farm utensils, and sometimes coins. My landlord at Kentville showed me a bright yellow *louis d'or* with the date 1704. It bears the clear stamp of the French king's profile and the lilies of France. This coin was discovered in a ploughed field, trodden out by the foot of an ox. What a story it might tell!

Peace now reigns where once the cruelties of war spread ruin and despair. For the parted lovers, and for all those who were torn from their homes in those long-gone days, all is ended, —

> "The hope, and the fear, and the sorrow";

but for those of us —

> "Who believe in affection that hopes, and endures, and is patient,"

this fair corner of earth will always be —

THE LAND OF EVANGELINE.

www.ingramcontent.com/pod-product-compliance
Lightning Source LLC
Chambersburg PA
CBHW030410170426
43202CB00010B/1557